MW00888323

YES!

There are many adventure books about treasure hunting.
But what about in real life?
Can you still find a treasure?
Are there real-life treasure hunters?

The answer is: Yes!
Let's learn about
the biggest treasures ever found,
and meet real-life treasure hunters!

THE VIKING TREASURE

In England there is a river called
the Ribble. By the river there lies
the village of Cuerdale.
An old legend said that anyone
who stood on the South bank
of the Ribble was within sight
of the richest treasure in England.
Some people believed it.
They looked for the treasure,
but never found it.

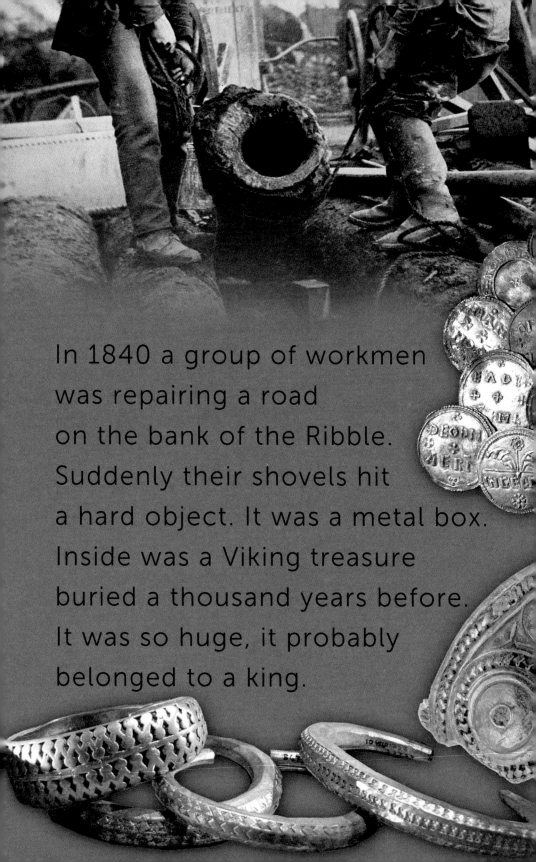

In 1840 a group of workmen
was repairing a road
on the bank of the Ribble.
Suddenly their shovels hit
a hard object. It was a metal box.
Inside was a Viking treasure
buried a thousand years before.
It was so huge, it probably
belonged to a king.

When they opened the box
the workers found silver coins,
Viking jewelry, and chunks of silver.
They gave the treasure
to the land owner.
He let each worker keep
one silver coin, and
gave the rest to Queen Victoria.
The treasure became known as
the Cuerdale Hoard.
Hoard is another word for
hidden treasure.

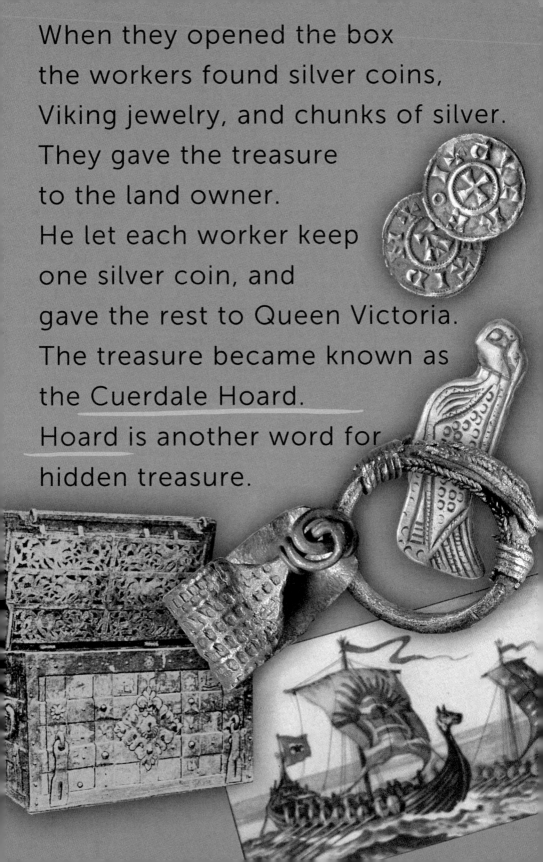

THE ROMAN TREASURE

In 1992 a farmer lost a hammer
when working in his field,
near the English village of Hoxne.
He asked a friend who had
a metal detector
to help him find the hammer.

A metal detector is an instrument
that can tell if there is metal
anywhere around.
You can often see people
with metal detectors
on the beach.
They look for
small treasures
in the sand,
like coins or
lost pieces of jewelry.

The farmer's friend started looking for the hammer with his metal detector.

Instead he found silver spoons, gold jewelry, and lots of gold and silver coins all over the field!

Ancient Roman coins!

The farmer and his friend called the police, and the police called the archaeologists.

ARCHAEOLOGY is a science that studies ancient cities and treasures lost and buried underground or under the sea.

Hidden in a wooden box, the Hoxne treasure was amazing: 569 Roman gold coins, thousands of silver coins, silver spoons, and Roman jewelry. The treasure was sent to a museum, and the farmer and his friend were paid for the treasure.

The Hoxne Hoard was buried
in the 5th century.
At that time England was part
of the Roman Empire.
But the empire was under
enemy attack from the North.
So the Roman army left
England to defend Rome.
The Hoxne treasure belonged
to a family who left for Rome,
but hoped to return soon.

*Roman Emperor Honorius
on a coin from the Hoxne Hoard
and the ruins of the Roman
Colosseum (Circus)*

*Roman
soldier*

THE BANKER'S TREASURE

Johan Lohe was a banker
in Stockholm, Sweden
in the 17th century.
Soon after he died,
Sweden was at war with Russia.
The Lohe family buried
some of his money in the ground
for safe-keeping.

In 1937 two construction workers found the Lohe treasure:
85 silver spoons, dishes, and cups, and 18,000 silver coins!

THE GOPHER'S TREASURE

In 2018 Russian archaeologists working near the city of Astrakhan, noticed that a gopher was digging a hole by their tent. Gophers build long tunnels underground where they store roots and grain for winter.

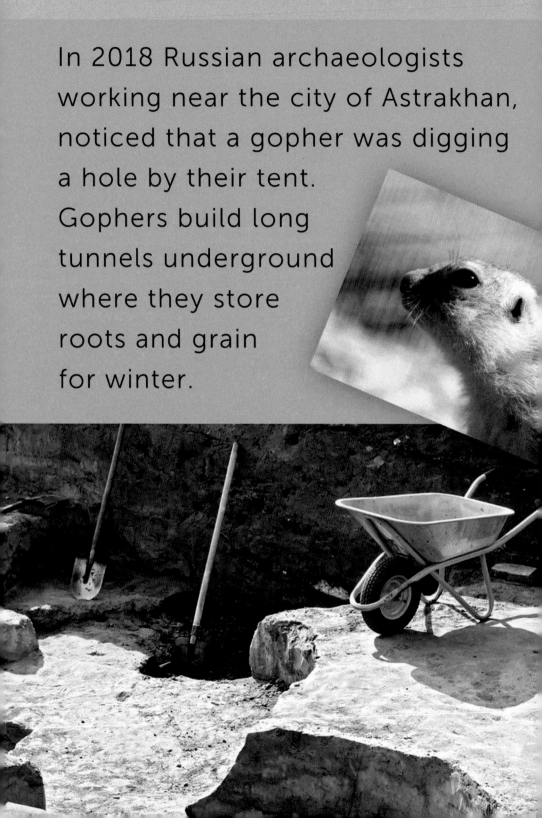

One morning the archaeologists
woke up and saw a pile
of silver coins by the gopher's hole.
The gopher had found a treasure!
But he didn't want treasure.
He needed room to store
his roots and grain for the winter.
So he threw out the treasure!

GOOD JOBS!

Archaeology is a good profession,
if you want to become
a treasure hunter!
Another great profession
to take you on treasure hunts is
OCEANOGRAPHY,
a science that studies the oceans.
Many treasures are found
in the seas!

UNDERWATER TREASURE

In 2015 two scuba divers found
a gold coin on the sea floor
near Caesaria, in Israel.
They looked around and suddenly
they saw lots of coins
shining in the sand!
They called archaeologists
and oceanographers,
who started digging...

Buried under the sand was
a whole big ship!
It sank around 1600 years ago.
The coins in the treasure were
from the time of
the Roman Emperor Constantine.
In those days people didn't have
scuba diving gear and couldn't get
sunken treasures back
from the sea.

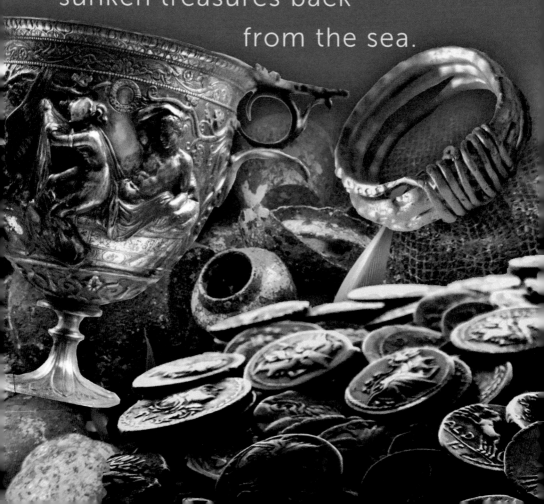

MODERN TREASURE HUNTERS

Today treasure hunters
use a lot of special gear
to look for sunken treasures.
They use
metal detectors,
scuba diving gear,
and remote-controlled
robots with cameras.
Let's meet some
of the best
treasure hunters!

LEE SPENCE

Lee Spence is an American treasure hunter. As a kid, he loved tales of pirate treasures and sunken ships.

He made his own diving gear and discovered his first shipwreck in 1959, when he was 12.

When he was 23 he found Hunley, the American submarine that was lying on the ocean floor for 100 years until Lee found it!

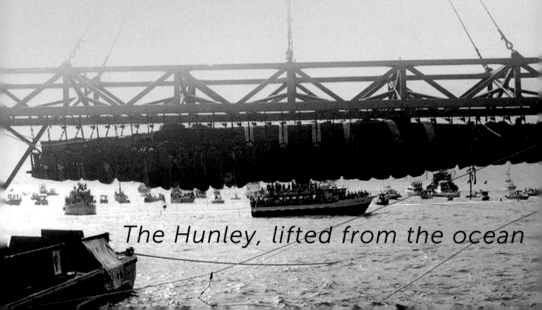

The Hunley, lifted from the ocean

THE PIRATE TREASURE

Captain Samuel Bellamy
was born in England in 1689.
His mom died when he was a baby,
and he became a sailor
as a teenager.
When he was 27 years old,
he left for America
to look for hidden pirate treasures.
But then he became
a pirate captain
himself!

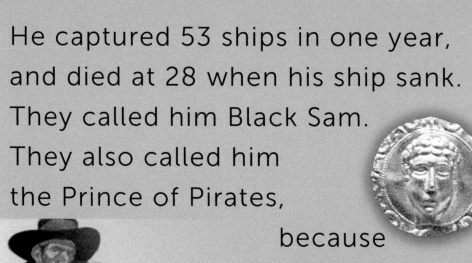

He captured 53 ships in one year, and died at 28 when his ship sank. They called him Black Sam. They also called him the Prince of Pirates, because he was nice. When he captured ships, he took their treasures, but never killed people who were on the ships.

In 1716, in the Caribbean sea,
Samuel spotted a ship that was
so fast and beautiful he wanted it
to be his own. That ship was the
Whydah, one of the fastest ships
of that time. Captain Bellamy
ordered his men to raise
the Jolly Roger,
pirate flag,
and chase
the Whydah.

The pirates chased it for 3 days before they came close enough to fire a cannon at the Whydah. After the first shot, the captain of the Whydah surrendered.
Take our gold, and let us go, he told the pirates.
But Bellamy didn't want the gold.
All I want is your ship, said Bellamy *let's exchange ships!* And they did.

Captain Bellamy had a girlfriend
who lived on Cape Cod.
He promised to show her
the Whydah.
But on his way to Cape Cod
a terrible storm crushed his ship.
It sank and lay in the ocean

In 1984 American treasure hunter
Barry Clifford and his his team
of divers found the Whydah and all
of Captain Bellamy's treasures.
The treasures were
5 tons of gold and silver.
The pirate ship was not far
from the shore,
but it was covered with sand.
Nobody ever found it
until Barry Clifford.

The Whydah treasure

Photo: Theodore Scott

In most places, you have to give
the treasure you find
to the country where it was buried.
But the court decided
that Barry Clifford could keep
all the treasure of the Whydah.
He could sell it. Instead,
Barry built a Pirate Museum
where you can see Captain Bellamy's
treasure and learn about pirate life.

THE SPANISH TREASURE

In 1804 a Spanish ship called
Nuestra Señora de las Mercedes,
which means *Our Lady of Mercy*,
was sailing from Peru to Spain.
It carried a huge load of gold.
When it was really close
to the Spanish coast,
an English ship stopped it.

The captain of the English ship
said the Mercedes had to go
to an English port for inspection.
The Mercedes was a big battle ship.
It had 36 guns. Its captain said: *No.*
Then the English ship
fired a cannon.
It sank the Mercedes with one shot.

The Mercedes lay
deep in the ocean until 2007

In 2007 American treasure hunter
Greg Stemm and his company
Odyssey Marine Exploration found it.
They kept their discovery secret.
Greg's team used robots
to explore the shipwreck.
Then they lifted the gold
from the Mercedes with a boat crane
and took it to the US.
But they couldn't keep this discovery
secret for long.

*The boat crane
the Odyssey uses
to lift treasures
from the ocean.*

Photo: Tim Green

The treasure was gigantic!
It was 17 tons of gold bricks,
and gold and silver coins!
When Spain learned about
the treasure, it said
the treasure belonged to Spain,
because the Mercedes was
a Spanish ship.
When Peru found out about it,
they said the treasure belonged
to Peru where it came from.

Greg Stemm
hoped that some
of the treasure
would be given
to his team.

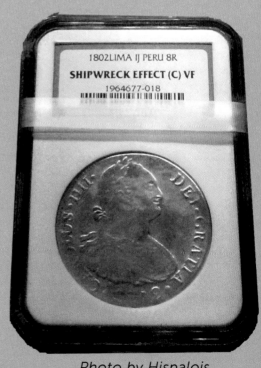

*A coin from
the Mercedes
prepared for sale*

Photo by Hispalois

But the court decided that
all the gold should go to Spain.
When the gold and silver
was mined in Peru,
Peru was a Spanish colony.
COLONY is a country
that is ruled by another country.
Peru was ruled by Spain,
so the treasure belongs to Spain,
said the court.

Coins from the
Mercedes treasure

Photo: Benjamín Núñez González

THE TITANIC

In 1912 the English ship Titanic,
the biggest ship of its time,
was crossing the Atlantic Ocean
on its way to America.
In the middle of the night
it hit an iceberg and sank.
For 70 years
nobody
knew
for sure
where this
happened.

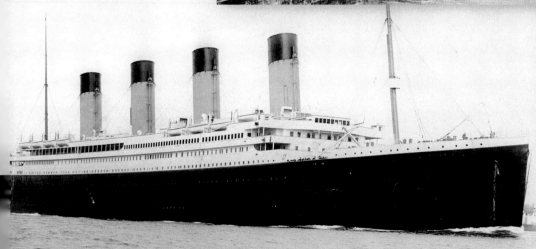

In 1985 oceanographer
Robert Ballard was on a secret
mission to find two submarines
that had disappeared in the Atlantic.
Instead of submarines, he found
the Titanic, two and a half miles deep
on the ocean floor!
The ship had split in two as it sank,
and it became clear that
it was impossible to raise it
from the ocean.

The Titanic,
70 years later

THE DEAD SEA TREASURE

The great news for treasure hunters is that there are lots of treasures that are still waiting to be found.

The Dead Sea is a salt lake between Israel and Jordan. The water of the Dead Sea is so salty, that plants and animals can't live in it.
That's why it's called the Dead Sea.

In the desert around the Dead Sea
archaeologists have found
many ancient documents.
One of them is the Copper Scroll –
a real ancient treasure map!
It is scratched on a sheet of copper
and has a list of 64 treasures
buried in Israel and directions
where to look for them.

For example, the treasure map says:

Treasure 3 In the cemetery,
go to the third row of stones.
You will find 100 bricks of gold.

Treasure 5 Go up the escape
staircase. On the left side,
two arm lengths from the floor,
you will find a bag of silver coins.

The problem is,
the map was made 2000 years ago.
The cemetery, the escape staircase,
and all those other places
are long gone. So far none
of these treasures have been found.
But one day someone will find them!